PRESIDENTIAL OVERHAUL

(IF YOU WANT ANYTHING DONE YOU HAVE TO DO IT YOURSELF)

RAY SANTOLI

ISBN: 978-1-4834-9460-9 (sc)
ISBN: 978-1-4834-9459-3 (e)

Lulu Publishing Services rev. date: 12/13/2018

CONTENTS

Presidential Overhaul (if you want anything done you have to do it yourself)

Here's my Presidential campaign ad for any voters who don't like to read (and no offense to them,
because I'm one of them). As for the rest of you,
I invite you all to read as little or as much of the
manuscript that follows this advertisement as the
content compels you to read.

"I don't know if it's true, but I've heard that due to
their obscene profits in the oil industry, there are
nations in this world that are able to send regular,
scheduled monetary gifts to their citizens, based
simply on the fact that those citizens happen to *be*
citizens of those respective countries. And apparently these same citizens are then able to live off of
those checks that they're receiving. To paraphrase
former All-Pro Chicago Bears linebacker Mike
Singletary, "I *like* that kind of party!" If I'm elected
President, there will be social, economic, and political reforms put into place that will hopefully pave

the way for the U.S. to join this Country Club-style fraternity of nations, thank you very much. And If such a proposition as this happens to sound appealing to any of you, then vote for Ray, because eventually it might literally *pay*!

This message was approved by Ray Santoli.

PREFACE

Apparently, quantum physicists have concluded that our universe is *probabilistic* in nature and that there's at least a mathematical chance of practically *anything* occurring. So, based on that supposition, I hereby stipulate that "omnipotence" from the standpoint of the third dimension might be able to be achieved by scientists in the future if they can figure out both how to achieve the quantum derivation of "all possible outcomes" for any given event, followed by figuring out how to impose the right amount and sort of force to whichever of the given available outcomes they might want to occur, and then to have their ensuing application of that force hopefully result in that event actually occurring.

Also, romantic couples would practically never bicker with one another if they had never had sex with one another at any point in time. This is due to my supposition that sexual intercouse produces negative emotions within the female of the species. I mean, how else could the female's lack of preoccupation with the human sensation of orgasm be reasonably explained?

Also, "nerdism" is the mildest form of autism. The term "nerd" has become a clinical term in the psychological community, and it generally denotes an individual who lacks the ability to grasp social cues. And autism is a disease of social disabilities. Also, autistic individuals often demonstrate exceptional cognitive abilities, and nerds generally have high I.Q.s. So, I suspect that there's a connection between the two groups.

And finally, if everyone were to make an effort to stop using offensive words, then those words would all likely die a natural death in only the course of time of one or two generations, because people aren't born knowing any words or their meanings. Individuals have to be continuously exposed to words for those words to have any meaning and for those words to be able to survive (I'm referring specifically to the "N" word here people, in case anyone out there's interested in eradicating it).

So, those are the only four major revelations that I've had since my last book, and as you contemplate the possible implications or ramifications of those revelations, I say to you, "Greetings, dear reader." This book is directed towards taking an informal examination of the office of the President of the United States, and what might be done (if anything) differently by a new or different holder of that office in regards to the array of tactics that the previous administrations have traditionally chosen to pursue in their attempts to improve the quality of life of the people "for which it serves."

Writing this is an odyssey for me because I don't know what my conclusions will be when it's all over, and I'm as curious as anyone to find out. But to start with, I have to first admit that I never thought that I would ever again have a book's-worth of information to share with anyone. But that assumption eventually fell flat under the weight of the continuous, unrelenting dissention that I've found myself having with basically *all* of the professional political commentators that I've been hearing from in this country, for basically the entirety of my adult life.

If all of our political policies made sense to me, and our all-around conditions were as good as could reasonably be expected, then I wouldn't have anything worthwhile to contribute on the subject of the Presidency. But frankly, I'm a little disappointed that we're not all enjoying a better quality of life and experiencing more security than we currently are here in America.

A President should want all of his or her (but for grammatical simplicity's sake from this point further I'll just be using the "male" gender designation in reference to the President) constituents to be able to live "the easy life", and he should want to protect them all from harm the way a mother hen does.

So, what more could be done to accomplish goals such as these? Join me on this, to borrow Einstein's phrase, "thought experiment", and as we go, I invite you all to ascribe either ridicule or creedence to any or all of my ideas as you may happen to see fit to do along the way.

INTRODUCTION

One day, years ago, I heard Arnold Schwarzenegger providing some color commentary during a prestigious professional bodybuilding competition that was being broadcast on t.v., and as I was listening to his comments, I thought to myself, "What a great job he's doing. Those are great industry insights." His analysis was extremely sharp. And over all these years, I've also found his cinematic acting to be quite "believable", as well.

But with that being said, and with no offense intentionally directed towards him, I've never heard an original political thought of his that contained even a *hint* of intelligence to it. I mean, I *did* hear him regurgitate some conservative rhetoric a couple of times over the years, but what fool couldn't do that? And the fact that his Austrian accent has failed to deminish even *one* iota over the course of his residence in the States suggests to me that he might be in possession of some sort of a learning disability.

Also, the fact that he's never admitted to using any steroids when questioned about having done so during his competitive bodybuilding career also suggests to me at least a *slight* character flaw on his part. I mean, even though the hundreds of competitors whom he faced and always happened to defeat in those bodybuilding competitions would now likely *all* be willing to admit that they themselves were *all* using steroids at the times of their defeats to him, we're supposed to believe that he himself was the only competitor who wasn't using any steroids, and that he was still able to develop better muscles than all of them? Give me a break. It's a ridiculous notion to entertain, if you ask me.

And while we're on the subject of "admitting to steroid use", this brings me to the case of one Ms. Martina Navratilova, who was always ranked around no. 12 in the world during the 1970's, and whose physique at that time resembled every other female player's physique in that sport, but in the 1980's she shows up with more muscle mass and a much more "veiny" look, and suddenly she becomes practically unbeatable up until practically the time of her retirement. It seems obvious to me that she started using steroids, but she has always denied it. I think that her steroid use was obvioius to Ms. Chris Evert Lloyd, too, but I'm guessing that Chris Evert had too much class to openly accuse her of using steroids, so, *Cheers to you, Chris Evert.* And then, in 2009, Martina had the unmitigated gall to publicly criticize other athletes who don't admit to using performance-enhancing drugs. Unbelievable.

Now that I've got all of *that* off of my chest, back to Arnold's political career: so, if *he* could be the Governor of arguably our nation's biggest, most wealthy, and most prestigious state (California) for several years without there ever having been any devestating major economic or social repurcusions resulting from it, then *that* fact alone tells me that the position of holding political office in this country has lost all credibility, whatsoever.

So f*** it, I might as well go for the gusto, too. I mean, my schedule's free, and maybe I could at least get a date with a young woman out of it if I happen to win an election. Plus, testing my political theories could easily become the determining factor in whether or not my life winds up being deemed to be one of abject failure or one in which my "adulthood-long string of losing" winds up being redeemed after all. Thanks for the inspiration, Arnold. "*I'll* run for President if you want, America. What the hell."

So, now that I've announced my candidacy, everyone can check out what I'm offering in the way of a political Platform. The following manuscript is basically a "long version" of the Platform that I would present to the American voting public in hopes of garnering their support for a Presidential run. I think it should also be mentioned that in addition to providing a lot of answers to any political questions regarding myself that anyone might have, this could also provide the voters with some measure of insight into my mindset, so as to familiarize themselves with me. So, "Thanks for your support!", in advance, and in the immortal words of Larry David, I hope everyone finds this book to be, *"Pretty, pretty good."*

INITIAL CONSIDERATIONS

I'm compelled to mention at this point that all of my books (including this one) are purely hypothetical (rather than scientific) in nature because I never do any formal research of any kind in support of any of the contentions or beliefs that I espouse in them. The *right* way for me to publish would be for me to test out all of my theories in scientific trials *before* I did any publishing. And I'm not contending that anyone such as myself who publishes without direct experience or research on a topic should be taken seriously. When a person writes without experience or research, he or she is just like a child doing a school writing assignment. The title of this assignment that I'm working on here could be, "What would you do if you were President?" But the fact that I'm writing this at all should show that I care, because I never liked doing any writing assignments in school.

But unfortunately for America, I'm not concerned enough with the welfare of my fellow man to the extent that I'm willing to invest the amount of time and effort that would be required of me to test out my theories before being willing to confidently implement them. And technological advancements and changes in social circumstances might likely occur over the course of the time that it would likely take to carry out such scientific studies, that whatever results and subsequent conclusions that might be drawn from them might likely be renderd moot, anyway.

Every human being only gets about "80 good years" in which to make a contribution to our society (or to any cause, for that matter). And I look around at almost everyone and I think to myself, "You call *that* a contribution?" I'm at least *cognizant* of the fact that my life's been a complete waste of time and that it will likely remain one. But what's everyone else's excuse who always wants to complain about the "dire" state of affairs that they're always claiming that we're up to our necks in? I mean, If you're not going to *do* anything about your problems just keep them to yourself, you crybabies. I mean, there are almost always opportunitiess for activism in anyone's life.

As far as I'm concerned, though, if there aren't enough desperate voters out there who feel like there's not enough time available for scientific testing, and that my ideas sound good enough to them, and that they're ready to roll the dice right now with a new, progressivley-minded candidate such as myself, then I invite anyone who happens to have the "appropriatly-minded" attitude for following standard scientific procedures to "experiment away" with any or all of the political ideas that I present in this book whensoever or howsoever he or she may choose, and for him or her to also, subsequently, do with the results whatsoever he or she will.

I, however, anticipate myself being either dead or having in some other way naturally succumbed to political disenfranchisement within the next thirty to forty years anyways, so in my mind, there's no real feeling of desperation for myself to get or to be involved in the political process anyway—I can either take it or leave it as far as trying to help out America is concerned. At least I'm offering my help right now while I'm still of "sound mind and body". And if getting elected doesn't happen to work out, I'll at least be able to live with myself by saying, "I at least offered some possible solutions, but not enough people saluted when I raised my flag, so what can you do?" And perhaps voters would be justified in withholding support from someone such as myself who lacks experience in shaping public policy, but at least my conscience will be clean after publishing this.

Another consideration in this whole proposal is the fact that in order for myself to run for President, I'll have to hopefully attract and then adopt a running mate, a.k.a. the Vice-Presidential candidate. And it therefore seems prudent to me at this time to both address and implement that process right here and now: first I'll provide my preferred qualifications that I would be seeking in a potential running mate. Then I'll provide what I hope would be attractions to a potential running mate that my envisioned style of management might likely offer to him or her. Then I would require of any qualified and interested parties for this position to then write a *brief* email to me at *santolirv@yahoo.com* addressing their qualifications and interests. And, if based on those qualifications and innterests, I were to then develop an interest in ourselves potentially teaming up together, then more substantial discourse could take place between us at that time. Incidentally, that email address is also the source for anyone who might be interested in acquiring a free electronic copy of this very book (but don't tell my pusblisher that!).

Since I don't have any political experience, I

assert that the Vice-Presidential *yin* to my *yang* do have some. I imagine that his or her given experience in this arena could easily become an invaluable asset to our cause should it ever happen to be determined at any point by our own confabulation that I might be politically "in over my head" in any particular official scenario/situation. Beyond that, I would ask an open mind, cordial demeanor, and a consciencious attitude of him or her, and that he or she provide constructive criticism whenever appropriate, and that he or she offer the traditional attributes of deference and helpfulness towards myself that have come to be expected of a second-in-command.

I suspect that there's a motivational element of ego gratification within many, if not most, of the people who hold positions of power. But ego gratification, of course, hasn't any place within the objectives of leadership, in my opinion. Preparing a replacement to experience success in one's own absence works against an ego-gratifying model of leadership, but a leader making an effort to make his or her potential replacement a success is perhaps the most valuable gift that a leader can bestow upon him or her.

Because I believe in grooming and empowering replacements, I hereby purport to present a novel opportunity in this country's history of Vice-Presidential service: I'd like to be able to offer the Vice-President the opportunity to take over as many of the day-to-day Presidential operations or activities as he or she would like to gain experience at doing. I don't personally have any burning desire to be involved in the day-to-day concerns of politics. My chief concern while in office would be in ensuring that the major reforms that I both promised and was elected to deliver to the American public would be enacted and fulfilled. And I would hope that my involvement or oversight of those particular reform projects would tend to be my main activity while in office. But imagine this, if you will: if I happened to trust the Vice-President to competently perform *that* function, as well, I might delegate *that* duty to him or her, as well, if the opportunity happened to present itself and the Vice-President happened to be interested in doing so. As far as I'm concerned, the Vice-President and I could ostensibly *switch roles* as long as I were confident that my agenda were still going to be fulfilled.

So, if based on the information that was just provided and also based on how agreeable you find the remaining information in this book, you happen to feel like you might be a good fit for the position of Vice-President in my (but as was just suggested, perhaps mainly *your*) Presidential administration, then email me and we'll try to determine how professionally compatible we might be with one another. But nobody please contact me who doesn't meet the following Presidential eligibility requirements: at least 35 years of age, lived in the U.S. for at least 14 years, and are a nutural-born citizen of the U.S.A.

Now, with all of that being said, I have to acknowledge the possibility, right up front, that

everything contained in this book might be complete hogwash; which would therefore necessarily
relegate this content to the category of "For what
it's worth". But, with that *also* being said, statements that are true *should* be written, no matter
how offensive they may seem to be to anyone's given
sensibilities, and statements that are false *shouldn't*
be written, no matter how appealing *they* may seem
to be to anyone's given sensibilities. And by that
standard of judgment I say, "You're welcome" for
any of the following insights that might happen to
be true, and "I'm sorry" for any of those that might
not happen to be.

OFFICIAL CONSIDERATIONS

From what I've gathered from my early education and from watching the news over the years, the President doesn't seem to have many official duties to perform. He's the Commander-in-Chief of the military, which I interpret as meaning that he has to decide on a daily basis on whom he's either going to "declare war" or not. And history suggests that *that* decision doesn't likely provide much work for him to do on a day-to-day basis.

Another of his duties is having to occasionally provide the "State of the Union" address. This is an assignment with no real definitive or concrete specifications to my knowledge, so there are presumably broad parameters for filling this bill.

Practically any comments regarding the country's current welfare would seem to qualify as satisfying this Constitutional requirement, so there isn't necessarily much work to be done there, either, if he's so inclined to not make a big deal out of that assignment, that is.

He's required to either sign or veto Congressional bills that cross his desk. Bills that successfully make it out of Congress are few and far between, so *that* duty shouldn't be much of a burden to him or a great time-consumer on his part. Are you starting to see my point here? If a President were so inclined, it seems to me like he wouldn't have much that he's required to do during his term in office.

To the extent that the Secret Service would deem it reasonable, I think that traveling around the country and having brief interactions with as many residents of the country as possible might be a fun, worthwhile agenda for the President to pursue. I mean, it's always a big thrill and a morale boost for anyone and everyone who meets the President. So, why shouldn't he spread the "socializing wealth" around if he isn't necessarily, as I suspect, beseiged by official duties? In this scenario, the President would be filling more of a role as a "Good-Will Ambassador".

What else? It also seems to me that every sub-ordinate level of government has been designed to handle every other need that the country might have. Hence the cliche, "Call your Congressman" whenever you have a problem. But I don't think there's a governmental position in place besides the President's that's designed to interact or make deals with leaders of other countries, so if the President is inclined to do so he could be the one to do that; though I could also envision him delegating much, if not all, of that power to the Vice-President or an ambassador, if he so chose. So once again, not much inherant work for the President to do on a foreign affairs level, either, "unless, of course, war were declared" (*Futurama* episode reference).

The President can provide pardons to criminals

if he'd like to, but this is an option and not a responsibility, as far as I know. So, once again, reviewing criminal cases wouldn't necessarily be a cumbersome burden to him if the mood didn't happen to strike him for it to be.

The President assigns several governmental and judicial job positions to people whenever he takes office or whenever a vacancy in one of those positions occurs. I don't believe he even gets the final say in the judicial positions. Congress has to *approve* those choices. And there aren't that many positions that he has to fill, so *that* process, as well, should take up an insignificant amount of his time relative to his four year term.

I have to assume that I'm failing to recognize some unbeknownst-to-me Presidential duties that would render my claim that the President isn't Constitutionally bound to any great work load, to be bogus. But until I become aware of such duties, I'll just plow ahead with my thesis.

JOURNALISTIC GRIEVANCES

However fit or unfit for their respective political positions history may end up deeming both Schwarzenegger and Trump, I'm proud of them both for grabbing the bull by the horns and trying to actually *do* something to help this country, rather than themselves having been content to simply criticize our state of affairs without ever offering any assistance to change our circumstances, as it seems that the rest of us are almost always content to do.

So, what is it, that everybody in the news media happens to *care* about all of our nation's problems, but it's just that none of the them ever happen to have any *solutions*? Is that what I'm to glean from a lifetime of hearing their endless chatter? I mean, if a reasonable person had any solutions, he or she would then try to *act* on them, right, instead of just continually running his or her mouth about them day after day?

I say let "big talkers" submit their doom-and-gloom predictions into a national database. But their predictions would have to include some means of identification, a measurable result, and a measurable time period by which the result would have to be rendered. And then I suggest letting whichever people make the most accurate predictions then be considered for governmental leadership positions.

The problem that I have with journalists is that they never *do* anything about the problems that they cover. "Thanks for sending reporters to crime scenes and devestated areas, though. That's really helpful" (sarcsm). And then we have to watch their egos inflate while they recite the news strories of the day, as if they're making some difficult and critical social contribution by doing so. I wish media companies would just let middle school students or an automated computer voice read the news, so that everyone would see how simple and meaningless it all is.

The "power of the press" is demonstrated whenever individuals or groups who have broken the law or told lies get their hands caught in the cookie jar, and then the press blows the whistle on them. I admit that journalists do worthwhile work when they uncover conspiracies and cover-ups, but the *impotency* of the press is demonstrated whenever they attack individuals or groups who are acting *within* the confines of the law, because all the journalists can do then if they don't like someone is spit into the wind due to their lack of political authority.

The "actuary tables" seem to predict that the journalism profession is good for uncovering a major cover-up or conspiracy about once per decade on average: the 1919 Blacksox scandal, Hollywood black-listing around 1950, college basketball point-shaving a couple of years after that, radio payola around 1960, perhaps the JFK assassination in the '60's, Watergate in the '70's, Iran-Contra in the '80's, perhaps Whitewater in the mid '90's, realease of Big Tobacco's internal documents in the late '90's, and possibly Hillary Clinton's release of classified documents and the Russian hacking of elections this decade. Please forgive me if I left out any of your favorites. You can be the judge of whether or not this track record of indictment merits all of the journalistic bluster that we've been continuously exposed to during our lives.

Here's one of the disagreements that I have with professional political commentators: they make a big deal out of the daily activities of the President; as if his general activities have a great bearing on the course and outcome of our daily lives or that of our nation. Allow me to make a couple of points or to provide some observations that I've noticed: I've been consciously aware of the effects that Presidential decision-making has had on this country since the Jimmy Carter administration. And one President's decisions and their consequential effects on *my* life have been indiscernable from any other President's decisions and *their* consequential effects on my life the entire time of that consciousness.

But could this perception of mine simply be "observer bias" on my part? Let's see if there's any scientific data to back me up on my claim that the Presidents during my lifetime have been effectively and essentiallly "interchangeable" from one to the next. Look at the major economic and social indicators during my conscious lifetime (again, since Carter): gross domestic product, unemployment rate, inflation rate, graduation rate, crime rate, mean family income, budget deficit, trade deficit, national debt, etc. Republicans and democrats claim to have significantly different methodologies in their respective political approaches to dealing with these issues, yet if one looks at the numbers, I believe that trends have remained relatively the same over the course of *all* of the different Presidential terms involved, and nothing ever changes.

If I weren't concerned about the effect that it

might have on "consumer confidence", I'd like to see how, if at all, the major economic indicators of this country would be effected by having a *chimpanzee* serve a four year term as our nation's Commander-in-Chief. I'm not kidding. I suspect that the way the office of the President has been managed over the past several decades completely lacks any economic or social impact.

It's ironically amusing to me that whenever children's schools hold in-school political elections, the teachers always make a point to dissuade the children from turning the elections into a "popularity contest". But I'd like to determine how political elections actually scientifically differ from popularity contests, because there definitely seems to me to be an element of sentimentality involved in the voting/election process. Look at how Presidential candidates almost always win their home states. Do the voters in candidates' home states always just agree more with the platforms of their state-representing candidates? That would be quite a coincidence, if so.

One day I'd like to see some candidate approach an election purely from the standpoint of a "popularity contest" and see how well he or she does. The results might be surprising. Along with admitting that elections are popularity contests, teachers might want to start admitting how important "who you know" is in determining success in one's life, as compared to the importance of simply "what you know".

EDUCATIONAL AND MILITARY REFORM
(BOTH ADDRESSED IN ONE FELL SWOOP)

Education is probably the most valuable tool at leadership's disposal in its effort to improve society. And it's with this belief and the following deeper perspective that we begin our foray into educational reform: there was modern weaponry, modern transportation, dense population areas, and criminal record keeping one hundred years ago, so let's just go back that far in our country's history—let's call it the *modern era.* Just between hospitalization records and separate reported law enforcement incidents (which means we're not including undocumented incidents), do you think that there have been roughly a million acts of violence purpotrated in this country every year during those past hundred years? I would bet, "yes". Now, is a hundred million incidents enough to inspire a determination for change in this country? Apparently not. And It's probably statistically as dangerous to live in America right now as it ever was. I'm going to propose some ambitious and untested policy changes in this book, but maybe the time is right for drastic measures, and the public is ready to gamble with its security.

There's very little in the way of concrete preventive measures in place to stop violence. There's a short waiting period for gun purchases, but I doubt that that significantly decreases the crime statistics. And felons aren't allowed to purchase guns, but I don't get the impression that that prevents any of them from acquiring any. The wealthy have more options at their disposal: they can try to isolate themselves in gated communities, heighten their home security measures, pay higher taxes to increase the police presence in their neighborhoods, hire body guards, move to cities with lower crime rates, etc. Less afflu-ent people can just arm themselves and pray, I guess.

The only *real* obstacles to one person's brutal-ization of another in this country are conceptual deterrents such as morality, punishment, and ret-ribution. Of these three deterrents, I get the feel-ing that it's much more the fear of punishment that motivates behavior than the other two; for which I commend our justice system's effectiveness. Fear of retribution and fear of punishment as motivators for an improvement in the population's civil behavior towards one another aren't worthwhile ideals in my eyes, though, as those motivations fail to edify. A different type of educational system could instill morality in our youth. Wouldn't it be great if school administrators and law enforcement officers rarely had anything to do with their work weeks because all of the children in their communities had been raised properly and there weren't many people run-ning around causing problems?

The following is what occurs to me as an appropriate Platform for achieving such a reality.

plank #1: Immediately transition our military from a human-based fighting force to a drone-based one. Current military personnel would be used to achieve and maintain this transition. This transition would greatly reduce the number of active U.S. military personnel, which would in turn greatly reduce tax payer burden. This should also reduce the number of U.S. military personnel casualties.

plank #2: A drone force would eliminate the need for further recruitment of active U.S. military personnel for several years. Not having to pay new recruits would tremendously reduce tax payer burden.

plank #3: Let our drones and long-range missiles be our military presence overseas. Withdraw as much of the U.S. human military presence from our foreign military bases as can possibly be done without jeopardizing our ability to utilize these strategic locations for

U.S. military supply access and deployment. Reducing U.S. foreign military bases to those of skeleton crews would tremendously reduce tax payer burden.

plank #4: Let our drones and long-range missiles be our military presence in our homeland, as well. Consolidate active U.S. military personnel in our homeland to as few a number of military bases as possible. This would allow all military bases that aren't being used in this consolidation process to be transitioned into public military-style boarding schools for any and all "parentally authorized" male children.

plank #5: Any and all active U.S. military personnel that happens to become displaced by the effort to reduce our human U.S. military presence would be encouraged to join these newly converted "base-schools" in some hopefully convenient capacity for themselves. This would provide the schools with military-minded and military-trained leadership.

plank #6: Provide military-style "tough love" to the students at these base-schools in order to "break their wills and then build them up". "Breaking their wills" would entail crushing any rebellious attitudes on their parts, the retention of which would hinder their learning processes. "Building them up" would entail creating an attitude of trust within them, which is a necessarry ingredient for cultivating their learning processes.

plank #7: Hire enough psychologists and/or psychiatrists at each of these converted base-schools to provide one hour of psychological therapy to each student per week. This would allow students to work through any "baggage" that they may have, as well as helping to make them all thoughtful and rational beings.

plank #8: Provide the appropriate number and type of classes in Psychology at these base-schools to enable all of the students to have achieved a degree in Psychology upon their graduations. This would ensure that the graduates have an understanding of human motivation and behavior, which would therefore enable them all to apply this knowledge to their own lives and perhaps to the lives of others, as per may be requested of them.

plank #9: Prepare a progressive Parenting curriculum at the base-schools that would be presented continuously and non-stop throughout the students' tenures at these schools. This would ensure that the offspring of these children would be raised properly.

plank #10: Include a military-style, exhaustive Firearm Safety and Proficiency curriculum for students who are deemed by the base-school's instructors to be worthy of inclusion in such a curriculum. When these students realize that they're being entrusted with the ability to both take and save lives, I think they will feel a natural compulsion to adopt an accompanying attitude and mindset of honor for such a responsibility [I offer the following observation as a basis for this rationale: despite military bases having always been simply *flush* with what is probably traditionally the highest crime-producing demographic in this country (18-25 year old males), I'm unaware of any high rates of criminal misconduct having ever been reported or recorded within the military communities/establishments of this country].

plank #11: Include a continuous and non-stop Pro-Morality curriculum for the students. This would likely instill and engender both respect and concern for their fellow man's well-being, thereby reducing crime rates; not to mention the mental health benefit that would likely result from the increased feeling of good will towards one another that a curriculm such as this promotes.

FOREIGN POLICY REFORM

After putting a little thought into foreign policy, I think I'm beginning to see how the game has been played, and potentially *misplayed*, as well. It would, of course, be ideal if America only made business deals with other countries that would turn out to be financially beneficial to us, but unfortunately, we're forced to think of national concerns other than simply our financial ones. Because theoretically, a whole host of concerns might develop if we were ever to lose the loyalty of another country. So we end up funding missions to other countries that are essentially the opposite of being financially beneficial to us.

Here's a question: what legal greivance could

the rest of the world take up with us if we were to become politically isolationist in our practices? I assert that it's no "crime against humanity" to become thusly directed. The other countries might suggest that we have a moral obligation to continue our global philanthropy, but I suggest that we shouldn't resume our global philanthropy until *after* we take a position of being at least *one* of the wealthiest nations on earth; which we likely could have already have achieved by now if not for that same history of commitment to global philanthropy and the other ill-conceived political decisions that we've likely perpetrated periodically over the course of that same time. I mean look at the size of our annual gross domestic product. We *should be* rich.

A likely better idea than that, though, for all parties involved, might be for the rest of the countries to jump on our bandwagon, so to speak, rather than oppose us in our isolationist stance. The rest of the world might be best served to make financial contributions towards completing our assention towards the top of the global wealth chain, so as to expedite our return to our roles as global Police Chief and the world's primary source for humanitarian aid.

Here's a "hardball" conjecture: the other countries need us more than we need them. Let's consider what might likely happen in a worse-case-scenario in which the U.S. became a 100% politically isolationist nation, which happened to result in ourselves effectively becoming politically alienated from the rest of the countries of the world. Let's consider the possible outcomes, again from a worst-case-scenario perspective, because that's what one must do when considering options and when engaged in the mapping out of a future course of action.

Worst-case-scenario #1: in a 100% isolationist scenario, the U.S. would become responsible for providing itself with every single need that it required. Do we have the resources to accomplish this? I say, "Close enough. Adjustments can be made in instances where we may be lacking the exact ideal resource." If this assumption is true, then the other countries would be left with no source of political leverage to apply against us. So, there shouldn't be any likely disaster awaiting us from that potential standpoint.

Worst-case-scenario #2: countries might feel compelled to engage in open, armed conflict with us because they might feel that we owe them security, or that we don't have any right to abandon their needs, or that isolationism makes us weaker militarily, or just because they in some other way take umbrage with our new attitude and policy of isolationism. Whatever the reason, would any possible combination of a single country or even the entire *world* for that matter, feel comfortable engaging in a military dispute with us when we have as many nuclear missiles at our disposal as we do? I would encourage the United Nations to discourage any governments from starting down that escalating path of mutually assured destruction. So, there's likely no military leverage to be found against us by other countries from this potential standpoint, either.

Worst-case-scenario #3: enemies of ours are left to the device of trying to get away with potshot terrorist acts against us, the specific perpetrators of which would be, hopefully for them, difficult for us to track down, which would therefore aid said guilty parties in eluding our ability to determine the appropriate level and placement of blame and retribution to ascribe to each act. But I don't believe such attempted acts of terrorism would have much chance for success here in America, because I suspect that an isolationist model of home security lends itself well to an increased ability for ourselves to provide for own protection, because there would be less unknown individuals and commodities entering onto our shores or through our borders. And we would also likely fortify our borders in this scenario, as well. So, if this were the tactic that were chosen/adopted by our opposition, then there would likely be no imminent large-scale terrorism threat looming over us from that standpoint, either.

Worst-case-scenario #4: it seems like I would be

remiss if I didn't include "nuclear holocaust" in a list of worst-case-scenarios that potentially involved global super-powers such as have been described. So there it is. Nuclear holocaust. Everyone loses. And even pointing the finger of blame would seem rather anti-climactic at that point, wouldn't you say? Let's hope that no leaders are ever forced to consider *that* as their best option.

So, what would the rest of the countries be left with, assuming that they decided to refrain from making a concerted effort to *forcibly* ruffle our feathers, but instead, rather, decided upon engaging in a resentment-based political and economic boycott of us, therefore leaving themselves without our involvement in their lives? They would then naturally find themselves without access to our trade goods, which they might likely find inconvenient and discomforting for themselves. They would then also naturally find themselves without access to our military influence in combating all of the bad actors/evil-doers of the world, which they also might likely find inconvenient and discomforting for themselves. And they would then also naturally find themselves responsible for providing humanitarian aid during disasters, which they also might likely find inconvenient and discomforting for themselves (if they even felt compelled to lend any aid at all, that is).

I don't think there's currently a formidable military threat to us in the world besides China (whatever "formidable" implies). Every other nation seems to be either too poor, or is lacking military might, or is simply a disinterested "third party". "Communist encroachment" may have been a legitimate reason for previous Presidential administrations to have abandoned any notions of U.S. isolationism, but I can't help but think to myself, "Enough of this scaredy-cat mentality." Let's put the ball in Red China's court and see where their ambitions lie. Do they really want to rule the world? Everyone knows that playing a game of chicken with the U.S. would be like a "...dance with the Devil in the pale moon light" (*Batman* movie reference) —not something you'd want to voluntarily agree to do. Only a madman would want to prove something badly enough to risk a nuclear exchange with us.

Would China take over the world if we withdrew ourselves from the global stage? If so, then that would imply that our current *presence* on the global stage is in some way serving as a deterrent against that particular desire of theirs; which would also mean that we're currently doing something to China that we wouldn't be able to do if we were in "isolation". I'm going to go out on a limb and say "bollocks" (*V for Vendetta* movie reference) to that premise. I suggest that nuclear missiles are the only deterrents that our country will ever need at any time and under any circumstances and against any foreign threat. Period. Ultron (of *Avengers* movie fame) couldn't access our country's nuclear launch codes, but the President can.

When a country has a stockpile of nuclear missiles and enough natural resources to be self-sufficient, then that country doesn't have to listen to *anybody, anytime, anywhere* until proven differently. And, who knows, if I were President I might even become interested in raising the stakes of armed conflict even higher than that—no more allowing the deaths of thousands of our young men in order to avoid nuclear escalation. Perhaps all of our soldiers' lives that have been lost in military conflicts in recent decades have been sacrificed needlessly. I don't like the idea of risking *any* American lives in armed conflicts. That's what the missiles are there for. I might only become interested in allowing *volunteer* soldiers to risk their lives in an armed conflict. And once the number of American volunteer soldiers were exhausted, then the conflict would immediately enter into the "nuclear option" portion of the program. "Say hello to my little friend!"(*Scarface* movie reference) and "Go straight to jail. Do not pass Go. Do not collect $200" (*Monopoly* game referrence).

I'm guessing that in exchange for not producing their own nuclear weapons, most countries have likely agreed to some deal with the U.N. to the effect that the U.N. promises to defend, by any means necessary, said countries from any potential occupation and overthrow by any foreign governments. So any time China wants to increase its territory, the U.N. would be under obligation to stop China. How? I don't know. But this is likely the deal that the U.N. made with these smaller countries in order to halt global nuclear proliferation; which makes sense to me, beause justifiably, the inhabitants of the Earth don't want to allow just *any* potential crackpot leader of *any* country to have access to nuclear missiles at his or her own discretion.

I sympathize with Alan Alda and his anti-nuclear demonstrations, but let's think of the alternatives. With technological advancements the way they currently are, I suspect that even an all-out, more primitive, *gun-powder*-based war could wipe out a billion people and cause generations-worth of damage. The threat of the use of nuclear weapons *does* seem to have reduced the number of casualties of war over the past, roughly, 75 years, wouldn't you say? The only problem is how those statistics would become inverted if the nuclear option were ever exercised.

Allowing arbitrary leaders of countries to be in charge of their own nuclear stockpiles leaves too much to chance, in my opinion. That's too much power for any one country to have. There should be oversight. That might be a good use of the U.N.: to somehow only allow a U.N. committee to authorize the use of nuclear missiles. I don't know what that oversight would entail, however.

A foreign affairs model that the U.S. seems to sometimes engage in and that everyone, including myself, seems to deem as commendable, is when the President sometimes takes a "moral high ground" stance in regards to other countries and their leadership. It's a scenario in which a country's leadership has to defend and justify any of their questionable political practices before our President agrees to do any business with them. And if any of their practices are found to be wanting, then some terms of agreement then have to be drawn-up in reference to those disagreeable policies that would need to be changed in order for business to be conducted between our two nations. And I would invite other countries' leaders to apply the same standards to us, as well. If another country has something that we want, yet they have a grievance against some part of our business model, then they should try to make us clean up our act before doing business with us, too.

To my way of thinking, I'd also be interested in meeting with any foreign leaders who might happen to show an interest in renouncing their own sovereignty and becoming, in effect, *adopted* by us. I'm pro-homoginization: I prefer cultural "melting pots" to cultural "tossed salads". In my mind, the best foreign country is one that wanted to become a naturalized territory of our own. Let's all speak English and receive the same education. I think we'd all get along better then.

PRISON REHABILITATION REFORM

I feel sorry for people in prison, but maybe that's just because no one has yet to commit a felony against me. I don't know how reasonable this sounds, but in principle, I'm partial to the prison model that was presented in the movie *Escape from New York* with Kurt Russel. Incidentally, I'd like for him to make a third "Snake Pliskin" movie before he gets too old. Same goes for you, Jim Carey, and your *Ace Ventura* movies. If the two of you can come up with a buddy movie that would kill those two birds with one stone, then that would be fine with me. Michael keaton's also great, so maybe make him the villain. There. You're on your way. Now just get your agents to arrange lunch together with the three of you so that you can all slap some movie together. I don't care how bad it is. I'm desperate to see it. Anyways, it couldn't be any worse than *Anchorman 2,* even if you happened to *try* to make a bad movie. In fact, it might be a worthwhile accomplishment if you *could* make a movie that were worse than *Anchorman 2* just because that would be such a difficult task. While on the subject of movies, I should also mention that the millions of people who constitute the poker community in this world are tired of waiting for *Rounders 2* to be made. Nobody's getting any younger here!

Back to business. I still suggest that there be conventional prisons for prisoners who misbehave while in prison or for any prisoners who happen to prefer "the institutionalized life". But for any prisoners who would prefer to try their hands at farming rather than rotting in prison, maybe provide them all with livestock and parcels of land in "securtiy fenced-in" areas of southern Alaska on which to farm. Doesn't Alaska pay people to move there anyways because it's so umderpopulated? Maybe provide them with building materials and tools with which to build frontier-style dwellings for themselves. Put shock collars on their necks with body cams attached to them so that monitoring their behavior and putting them back in cells would be easy to do should the need to do so ever happen to arise. I'm hoping that such an opportunity for partial freedom and activity, plus the hopeful fact of presenting them with a rather purposeful existence would provide enough incentive for them to rehabilitate themselves.

UNEMPLOYMENT REFORM

I'm super-proud of people who are willing to work for a living. The amount of time and energy that this country's workers dedicate to their jobs is staggering to me. To aid this instrumental ingredient in our economy, I'd like to see if an improvement in this country's Re-employment System could be achieved by converting the personnel in this particular governmental agency from those of "facilitators" to those of "recruiters". I'd like to see unemployment offices become manned by locally experienced experts in the most popular and in-demand job fields of their areas. These expert recruiters would personally know who the potential employers are, where to look for job openings, how each particular business in that field works; plus they would have an intimate understanding of all of the different job positions that coinside with each business, and they would likely be able to quickly assess potential workers' general utility levels so as to continue to expedite the re-employment process.

To incentivize these expert recruiters, whenever they would happen to achieve a successful job placement, as long as that placement continued to work for his or her new employers, these recruiters could receive all of the unemployment benefits (checks) that each of those particular re-employment applicants would have been given. So, the recruiters would basically be working on commision.

GUN CONTROL REFORM

What a mess this whole gun control issue is. It's kind of like the Healthcare and Social Security issues (which I don't happen to have any strong opinions about at this time). When roughly 500 people were shot in Las Vegas by a lone gunman in 2017, I would have bet that that incident were going to prompt the enactment of some sort of a ban on guns by our government. I said to myself, "If this incident doesn't prompt new gun control laws in this country, nothing will." So, apparently, "nothing will". What I actually observed, politically speaking, as a result of this massacre was that, of course, everyone was outraged and devastated by the incident, but the legislative needle didn't even happen to jump at all as a result of it. So, it appears that gun laws in this country won't be changing any time soon.

I'm personally a fan of the idea of there being a "great equalizer" such as guns available to the weak and strong alike in this country in order for everyone to be able to protect themselves and their property and also other people. Especially after the volume of information that's being released by women in the #MeToo Movement, which seems to indicate or reveal that practically every woman in this country has at some point been the victim of some form of sexual harassment or sexual assault by a man. And also that practically every heterosexual man in this country has at some point in time engaged in some form of sexual harassment or sexual assault towards a woman. Such revelations regarding the reality of our society can make a person reconsider his own mindset. I mean, am I the only heterosexual man who isn't sexually assaulting women? And if so, does that make *me* the abnormal one? I mean, what's wrong with me? Why won't I get off of my butt and start harassing women? Maybe I need to start psychological therapy in order to change this warped respectful attitude of mine that I have towards women. Just kidding. One thing you should know about me is, "I gots to tell jokes." I hope everyone out there can still take one.

Back to gun control: what does anyone who's ever been the victim of an attack usually say? Do they express wishes to have had a gun in their hands at the time of their attacks? I'd assume so. If non-lethal deterrents such as pepper sprays and tazers and maybe even some sort of "knock out" gas pellets were ever to become as completely effective as guns at incapacitating individuals, then maybe it might then become easier to convert our society away from its fondness for the use of lethal force, but until that time comes, maybe we should all just focus on improving our own personal body armor protection. And become like *Iron Man*, for example. Maybe that's where we're headed.

CAMPAIGN FINANCE REFORM

I'm hoping to re-write the book on political campaigning with this manuscript by taking advantage of the electronic age in which we live, and hopefully, thereby, enabling myself to campaign for President on a shoestring budget. This message of mine to the voters is able to reach them electronically via email, which happens to be a free service, and if I campaign as a "write-in" candidate, I would just have to find about 11 people on average from each state to represent me as an *elector* in case I should happen to win a state's popular vote in the election. And if anyone out there would like to represent me as an elector from his or her respective state, I would appreciate it if you would emaiil me your name and address, and I'll start a list that would then be mailed to your state's office of elections upon its completion. My email once again is *santolirv@yahoo.com*. And I don't think that there are any standards or qualifications that have to be met by anyone in order for one's self to act as an elector, except for maybe being an adult and a citizen of this country. You'd probably have to sign something eventually if I were to win your state's popular vote. "Ooh, look at this: I'm writing my first *interactive* book!" So, you can see how this particular approach to the election process could potentially minimize the financial burden that would be associated with myself running for President.

I'm going to take a page out of the ancient Greek philosopher Plato's playbook now and say that politicians shouldn't be paid. Much worse, they shouldn't accept campaign contributions from known individuals or groups. Plato recognized how money and favors invite corruption. I'll go ahead and say right now that if elected, I'll renounce my salary in some way (maybe by donating it to charity so that I'd be able to keep the retirement or social security portion of it. I would probably have to work out the details with an accountant). I mean, the President gets free meals, free housing, free transportation, and free medical care anyways, so it wouldn't really matter if he didn't have any money, right? Besides, I could just get a collateral loan by putting up any Presidential artifacts that I might happen to come across during my residence in the White House, right? Again, just kidding.

Here's an alternative option, though: upon possible voter consideration and approval of an option of having a "hands off" President (*a la* the "chimpanzee" model that I suggested earlier), I could simply agree to be a "less government"-type of President for the duration of my term in office by trying to interfere as little as possible with the countries activities, which might have the effect of allowing the country to flourish.

A pre-election poll could be taken of the

American voters as to which version of leadership they would prefer of me: the "go for broke" model that I've been steadily outlining and proposing in this book, or this "chimpanzee/hands off/less is more" model that I could also endorse. Personally, I could live with either one. And I could just simply agree to adopt whichever model happened to win the poll. But here's a rather incidental stipulation in my eyes: the only reason that I would ever agree to forfeit my salary as President would be as a gesture of good faith towards the American public; the purpose of which would serve to illustrate how I were only serving the *people's*, not my own, best interests with my reform initiatives. If I weren't going to have to engage in any initiatives, then any "good faith" gestures on my part would be evidenced by my *lack* of political activity, which would be easy for the public to monitor. And without the question of "the motivation" behind my decision-making ever needing to be therefore placed into question, I wouldn't see any potential conflict of interest in myself accepting a Presidential salary. So, maybe in this "poll scenario" I'd be secretly hoping to become the "Chimpanzee President" so that I could have some spending money (not really).

RELIGIOUS REFORM

I want Christians and voters alike to discover that there aren't any imposed limits on the range of freedom, power, and opportunity that individuals in this country possess in their religious and political expression. Our freedom, power, and opportunity for individual expression in this country extends beyond what the leaders of these two institutions have traditionally offered to us. I contend that the institutionalization of religion and politics in this world has had the cumulative effect of rendering the individual man's ability and right to make the Church and State a true reflection of his own core faith and beliefs, impotent.

It's time for individuals to take back the reigns

of power from the Church and State. There aren't any inherent authorities in this world who have the mandate to tell anyone how these two institutions are supposed to *be* or what they're supposed to *do*. The will of the people should be the only determining factor in deciding that.

Now, one thing that I hope voters in this country would like to experiment with for at least a *couple* of years if I were to take office is a ban on professional Christian preaching in this country. I think if preachers weren't getting paid, then they wouldn't feel so obligated to monopolize the Christian conversation. In fact, the fact that they *wouldn't* be getting paid might actually *increase* their motivation to become more taciturn. I believe that if Christians begin through their own personal Bible study and reasoning with one another, to decide for themselves (without leaving it to a "preaching surrogate") how to manage their own Christian lives for themselves, a great stride will then be made by them in the advancement of the Christian cause. One that, in my opinion, has been hundreds of years overdue. My rationale for this belief and confidence in this particular reform is drawn from the "work out your own salvation with fear and trembling" Bible verse.

I suspect that an additional benefit to facilitating dialogue amongst the Christian priesthood (which includes *every* Christian according to the Bible) would be the potential for the attainment and fulfillment of a deeper relationship between at least *some* Christians with one another, that could hopefully come to mimic the devotion and sharing that has traditionally been reserved for only the institutions of marriage or the most intimate of families. If any Christians were ever able to discover any fellow Christians with whom their attitudes were found to be completely compatible with one another, then those Christians could experiment with joining into a "brother" and "sister"-type relationship with one another, in which they shared their money and possessions with each other without hesitation or reservation, because they felt like true family members with one another. This is a model with Biblical precedence, by the way, and I think that the Bible intended for Christians to become *like* this, if not even *greater* than this.

As far as enforcing a ban on professional Christian preaching is concerned, I think that law enforcement could likely just use the same tactics that they use for tracking other types of illegal money transfers, and that they could use the same methods of infiltrating groups and setting up sting operations that they traditionally use to facilitate their process of collecting evidence. And ironically in this scenario, any preachers who might feel compelled to take a "civil disobedience" stance in defense of their chosen profession, might soon find him or herself preaching in prison for, God forbid, *free*!

I wouldn't mind any Christian preachers collecting "unemployment checks" or receiving financial support from a church group during this ban, as long as he or she refrained from doing any sermonizing during any period in which he or she were receiving said financial support. I know that this is a wild policy to suggest, but I would simply ask for the voters' trust on this issue. And it would likely only take a couple of years for Christians to decide whether to embrace or reject the premise of the experiment, after which the ban could immediately be lifted.

I've always heard preachers *talk* tough about Christians being able to endure religious persecution. If it turns out that preachers have trouble practicing what they preach in this instance, I think that that fact alone could serve as validation of my suspicions regarding the illegitamacy of their chosen profession. And also by protesting, they would likely be simply revealing themselves to be nothing more than typical lying politicians whose only real interest is in retaining their money and power. I mean, if their profession is legitimate, shouldn't they be confident that my proposed experiment would quickly fail?

DRUG POLICY REFORM

Writing this chapter will have its enjoyable mo-
ments for me because I'll get to write about a rather
newfound hero of mine. He's the only person to
whom I've ever applied the term "hero". And he's
also the only person in my lifetime who could have
inspired me to vote for him for President. I guess
Jesus qualifies as my hero, too, but I've never used
that term in reference to him before. Speaking of
"The Messiah", I never thought that I would ever
use *that* term in reference to anyone else for the rest
of my life, but it occurred to me while I was listening to this aforementioned hero of mine lecture that
he's actually "The Messiah of Human Secularism".
I also noticed that while I was listening to him for

the first several times that he was actually "blowing my mind" with the content of his lectures. And as this was happening, I thought to myself, "Has anyone else in my life ever blown my mind like this before?" And I concluded that the only other time in which that might have occurred would have been when I was considering the content of Jesus' message. But because Jesus' message is so familiar to us all here in America, I guess that I always happened to just take it for granted that it was a mind-blowing message.

Anyways, I'm doing a good job of keeping you all in suspense about who this mystery hero of mine is, aren't I? I'm wondering if any of you have already correctly guessed his identity. OK, I'll let you off the hook...It's *Terence McKenna*! I'm guessing that there's 100-200 hours worth of separate lectures of his available on the internet for anyone who might be interested's consumption. Maybe there's one or two of his lectures out there that I myself haven't heard. And I envy anyone who gets to hear him for the first time, even though he *does* have a rather odd-sounding speaking voice.

McKenna expanded my horizons on a multitude of subjects, and one of them was the topic of psychedelic drugs. I'm a curious person by nature, so I would naturally be interested in experiencing any relatively safe, new experience that the world might have to offer me (such as doing psychedelic drugs), but due to my Christian aspirations/committment, I've kind of "sworn off of" some activities that might be contraindicated by the precepts of the New Testament of the Bible; meaning that I'll likely leave my curiosity unsatisfied in the instance of doing psychedelic drugs. But that doesn't mean that McKenna failed to convince me of the value that psychedelic drugs might potentially offer for humanity.

Thanks to guinea pig states like Colorado, an emperical examination of marijuana legalization is currently taking place in this country. And I don't anticipate any major problems being discovered from the data that's being collected in regard to this examination. And with the assumed proportional reduction in the number of potential criminal prosecution cases and incarceration sentences that would presumably take place as a result of this decriminalization of marijuana, a commenserately smaller portion of State and Federal budgets would have to be allocated towards running criminal courts and prison facilities. Ergo, marijuana legalization will save a lot of money.

And due to the windfall of job creation, business profits, and taxable income that's accompanying legalization in these guinea pig states, I anticipate marijuana becoming legal almost everywhere in the U.S. before very long. And that prospect doesn't bother me at all. But thanks to Terence McKenna's influence on me, the drug crusade that I'm particularly interested in being a part of in this country is the one in which the legalization of psychedelic drugs takes place as quickly as possible. I'll leave it to McKenna's lectures to supply you with all of the details as to why this might be an attractive social movement or cause.

As for the rest of the controlled substances, the *idea* of legalizing them all is appealing to me if for no other reason than that it might lead to the end of their illegal sale and distribution in this country; which by extrapolation, therefore, might possibly put an end to the criminal mentality that is necessarily cultivated within individuals as a result of their involvement in this criminal enterprise. I mean, drug dealers and drug cartels are a savage lot to my way of understanding. The use of extreme measures on the part of our government to rid our society of their presence is a consideration that I don't necessarily find off-putting in the least. But due to the pernicious nature of opiates, I don't foresee a reasonable circumstance in which *they* could ever be legalized.

LABOR REFORM

Jobs are curious things. Nearly everyone who has one is frustrated by it at least *some* of the time, but nearly everyone would go *crazy* if they didn't have one and were then left with too much idle time on their hands. The secret would be to find something productive or engaging to do with one's down-time, I'd assume. But can people effectively fill a life-time's worth of down-time? I'm curious how all of the individuals in this world who don't happen to work are able to spend their days without losing their sanity.

The way our society is set up, as long as all of our goods continue to be bought and our human services continue to be paid for, this country should be OK. And It currently happens to be the case that humans are still intimately involved in the production phase as well as the consumption phase of this cycle. But I'm sure that everyone can envision an upcoming time when our society will be capable of completely automating its labor force. And I say, "Here! Here!" for that day because I'm pro-leisure: I'm in favor of a society (and entire world, for that matter) in which everyone were free to pursue their passions to their hearts' content. But even though a human presence might not ever be needed in the workplace of the future, I suggest that we always allow enough room for humans to occupy or create whatever spaces they may happen to wish to fill inside the labor force, simply for their own good health's sake.

A problem that might occur if our country were ever to become rich like some of those oil producing countries (but with the given stipulation in this case that it were to happen before the complete automation of the workforce had occured) would be a lack of incentive for our own citizens to become professionals at either challenging jobs like doctors and emergency "first responders", or certain menial labor-type jobs that lack fulfillment. In such a circumstance, we might be forced to allow our country's population to swell due to the necessary recruitment of poor immigrant workers to our shores who would be hopefully willing to do those jobs. Or failing that, we would have to somehow provide additional rights and privileges to any of our own citizens who might be willing to take on those roles.

THE REALITY OF POLITICAL ENMITY

Political solutions are designed to produce quick, favorable results, but the inherant risk involved with them is the potential opposite effect of what the implementation of an ill-conceived policy could have on whatever issue is trying to be addressed. Political solutions are generally weighed against technological solutions, which are traditionally slower in their approach than political solutions, but seem to always eventually fit in. This brings me to the dilemma of trying to all-but-eliminate our nation's dependence on foreign oil. We could immediately turn our nation upside down by mandating that all new cars be equipped with alternatively-powered engines, but consumers might balk at purchasing them for whatever reason, which could devestate that vital economic industry. Plus, who knows if a new technology is around the corner that's going to make internal combustion engines obsolete, which would necessarily render any long-term investment in alternatively-powered engines therefore obsolete, as well. But I say, "Damn the torpedoes! Full speed ahead!"...*with political solutions*, that is. You only live once. And I don't want NATO to get one more dime from us than we have to give them. We don't owe them anything.

This brings me to the realization that anyone, anywhere in the world who may happen to ever incur practically any negative result in his or her life might deem the President as having been responsible for that negative result. Or how anyone, anywhere in the world who may happen to disagree with any of the President's reforms during his term in office might deem him as being worthy of assasination. And the threats would be even more extensive than that: the President presents himself as an attractive, high-profile target for any criminally psychotic individuals out there, as well. Not to mention any of the pre-existing terrorist groups who already consider any U.S. President their sworn, natural-born, mortal enemy. The "honor and privilege" that accompanies becoming the President is reminscent of how military recruiters tell 18 year olds about all of the benefits of joining the military, but at the same time always happen to fail to mention to them how if they ever happen to get captured by the enemy after they join, they'll likely be tortured and/or killed.

INFORMAL FEDERAL BUDGET FORECASTING

Let's look at some possible best-case-scenarios for my proposed reforms: if a tremendous reduction in the number of active U.S. military personnel were to somehow be sustainable for several years without incident; and a policy of 100% American isolationism, in which a big percentage of the money that consumers spent on automobile fuel for several years went solely to American-owned companies and we didn't send out aid to other countries either during those years; and the legal purchase of marijuana were taxed throughout practically all of the states; and there were a reduction in U.S. prison

populations due to drug policy and education reforms, there would soon be a huge surplus in our
budgetary revenue that could be used to first pay
off our national debt, and secondly, after however
many years it might happen to take to do that, revenue could start going back to taxpayers so that they
could hopefully start living that country club life-
style that I mentioned in my campaign ad at the
beginning of this book. I mean, if these programs
that I've suggested were to be even *halfway* successful, I think an administration such as that would
have to be credited with accomplishing at least *fifty
times more* than any other Presidential administration in living memory ever accomplished, wouldn't
you say?

FINAL CONSIDERATIONS

I grant that helping the needy is a beautiful senti-
ment, but helping individuals is inefficient. A small
number of needy individuals could easily suck out
all of one's time, energy, and money and still come
back asking for more. Even in a best-case-scenario
where a person started out at a young age, and
had nothing but free time and a lot of money to
spread around, in how many lives could such a
person truly make a permanent change (assuming
that he or she only concentrated on helping *individuals* during all of that time, that is)? Granted,
thousands, I'd presume. But you can see what I'm
getting at here. I think the right political policies
could permanently help *billions* of people. And in a

best-case-scenario, it might only take a generation or two to do so.

If the voting populace feels that this country's political policies haven't done justice to the opportunities that have been afforded us here in "the land of plenty" and "the land of opportunity", and that leadership has essentially squandered the "blessings of liberty" that this country has bestowed upon its population for the past 200 years, then maybe out of a justifiable sense of guilt towards our inheritors, or maybe even out of a sense of ill-will towards the legacy of our political leadership, the voters might be willing to take a less measured, more results-oriented tact towards directing this country's future, and might, therefore, be willing to take a chance on adopting my proposals/measures.

This country's politicians and I have opposing viewpoints regarding the recommended actions that should be taken to improve our citizenry's quality of life. We both can't be right. In practice, one methodolgy would necessarily have to prove itself to be either inferior to or superior to its counterpart—either my ideas are retarded or theirs are. But the stakes in such an experiment between two competing doctrines would be high, and there wouldn't be any shame involved if the voting public felt compelled to simply maintain the status quo and the relative predictability that ostensibly accompanies it. Again, only a "gambling" voting population could feel compelled to experiment with *my* political proposals, and I don't feel like I have much at stake in either the "status quo" or the "gambling" scenario, so frankly, I'm not particularly interested in influencing any of the voters towards either point of view.

My proposals speak for themselves. They're there if anyone wants to implement them. It doesn't have to necessarily be myself who does it. But if the voting population expressed a "voting majority" desire for *me* to do it, I'd imagine that I'd go for it, even though I also imagine that the incumbent and ensuing "weight of the world" that would necessarily fall upon my shoulders following my adoption and embarking on such a mission isn't something that I would ever relish; as I assume that such a great insertion of stress into my life would necessarily prove to be detrimental to my mental and physical health.

Philosophy tends to be a "big picture", "large scale", "long view" type of construct. And because my thoughts and conerns in life tend to scew that direction, I suspect that I'm a rather philosophical person. And philosophical people will be drawn towards philosophical projects. And if there's a bigger opportunity than the office of the President of the United States for being able to embrace and engage in "philosophical activism" (did I just invent a new phrase right there?), then I'm having trouble thinking of one.

So, it shouldn't come as a surprise to anyone that my own personal gaze should turn towards the office of the President. But I realize that it's a lot easier to fantasize about turning philosophy into reality than it would be to actually try doing it. So, being the President wouldn't be something that I would be itching to do. It's too daunting. And boy would I want the world to pray for me if I ever actually *did* get voted in. And along with that, I would request that those prayers include requests that "no major crises" occur, either, during the course of my administration, please and thank you.

And *if* I ever did become President, and *if* my administration were to somehow be successful in its political and social reforms, then I would necessarily have to acknowledge the fact that the people who elected me and the workers who actually *did* the work of implementing my reforms would deserve most of the credit for those successes, because it would have been such a risky move to have elected me in the first place, and of course, nothing can be accomplished without the hard work of the people.

Let's hypothetically give myself the benefit of the doubt that the premises of these political and social reforms that I've suggested and roughly laid out here are sound. Even so, "the Devil is in the details".

So, the reforms couldn't be accomplished without everyone's help. The *people* make everything work in this country, not the President. And as the Bible says, God can have all of the glory. Amen.

ABOUT THE AUTHOR

Other titles by this author: A Better Brand of Basketball, In Pursuit of Perfect Poker, The Logical Approach to Christianity, Rebirth of Pragmatism (The Book on Fun)